SUNRISES

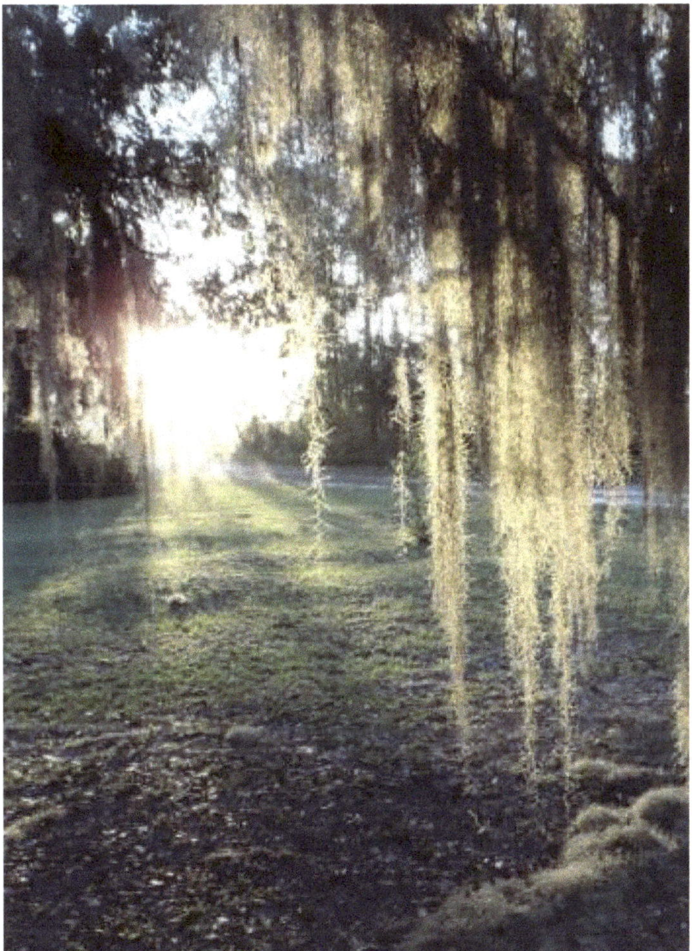

Photos and text by Henry Intili

1

Sunrises

Copyright 2022

Henry Intili, Bainbridge GA

The photos in this book were taken with my I-phone 10 or with our small Rocoh camera. No fancy or professional level equipment was used. (I don't have that stuff anyway).

PART ONE:

SUNRISES IN BAINBRIDGE, GEORGIA

PART TWO:

SUNRISES AND MORNINGS ELSEWHERE

Every morning it doesn't rain I walk the length of this dirt road from our house and back for a total of about one mile. I gather my thoughts for the day and photograph scenes that say something to me. I have always been a morning person. I long to greet the sun and welcome him to a new day.

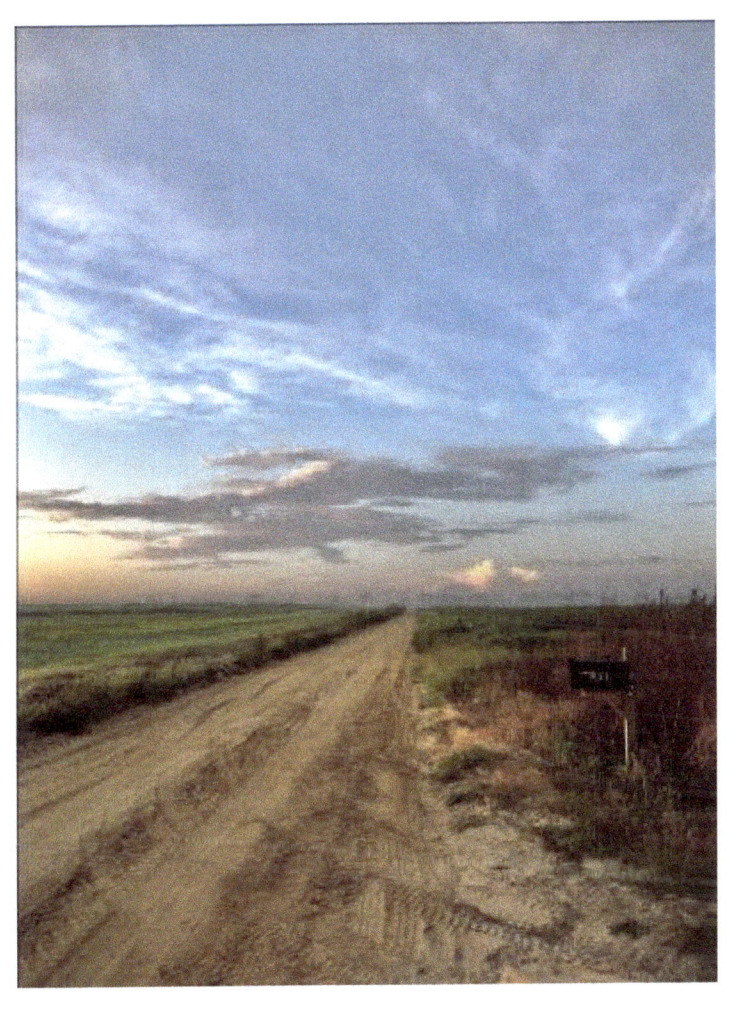

Mock Cemetery Road, September

A morning mist lies over our lawn and pond with its drowned oaks. The rusted iron dragon bell that we found in a small shop in Wales beckons me to breakfast. A fitting start to a foggy Halloween morning.

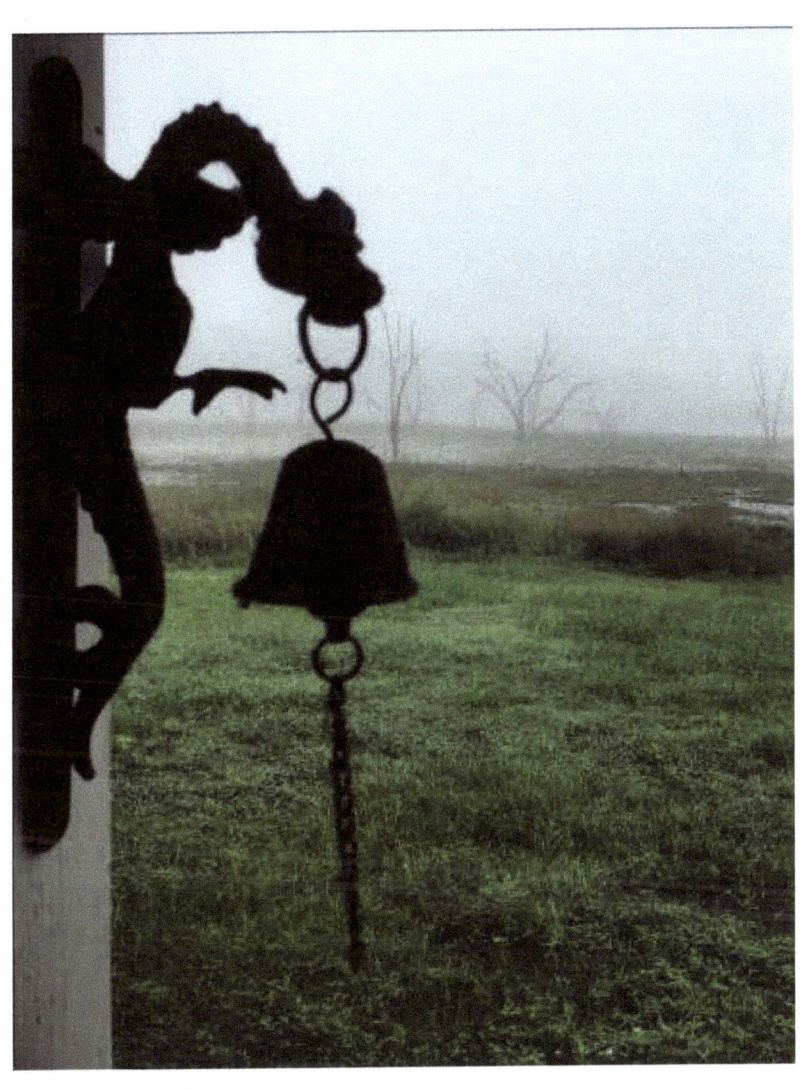

Dragon Bell and Our Misty Pond

On a clear morning the sun rises through sleeping tractors and harvesters in the peanut field. By mid-morning when the sun burns the dew off the plants and ground, the farmers bring the machines to life.

Harvesting Peanuts

I call these beauties "trumpet" flowers. They announce the dawn to the flowering cotton field with their heralding brassy music: *Wake up! Savor the sunshine!*

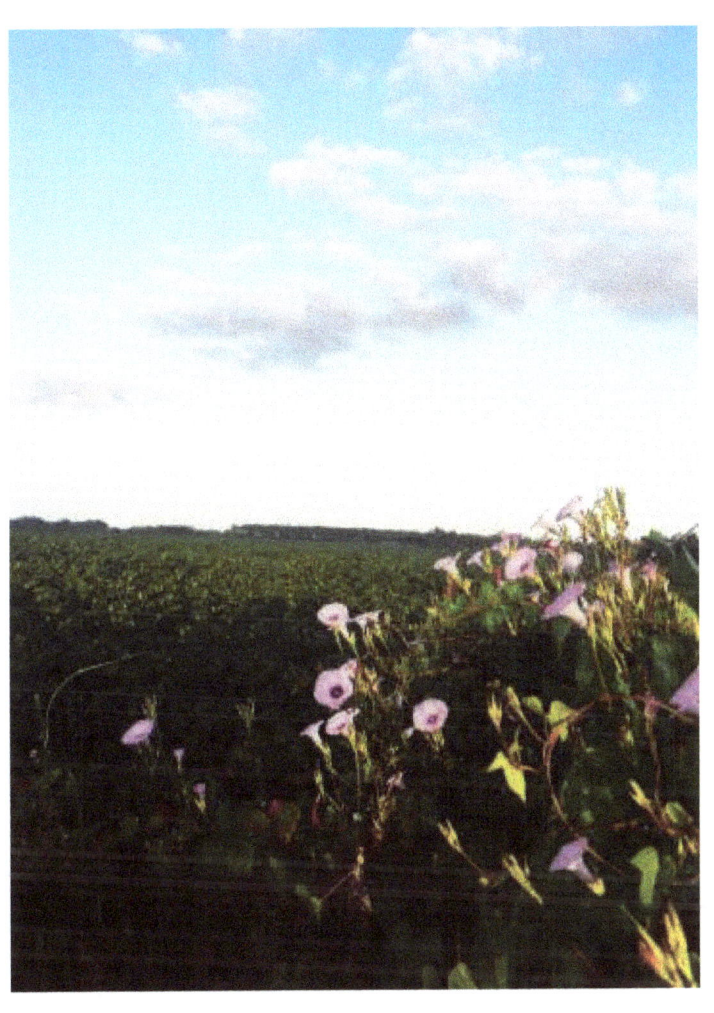

Trumpet flowers on the roadside

Many humid mornings in summer when the temperature is in the mid-70s and the humidity much higher the fields are covered with a blanket of mist that dissolves with the sun.

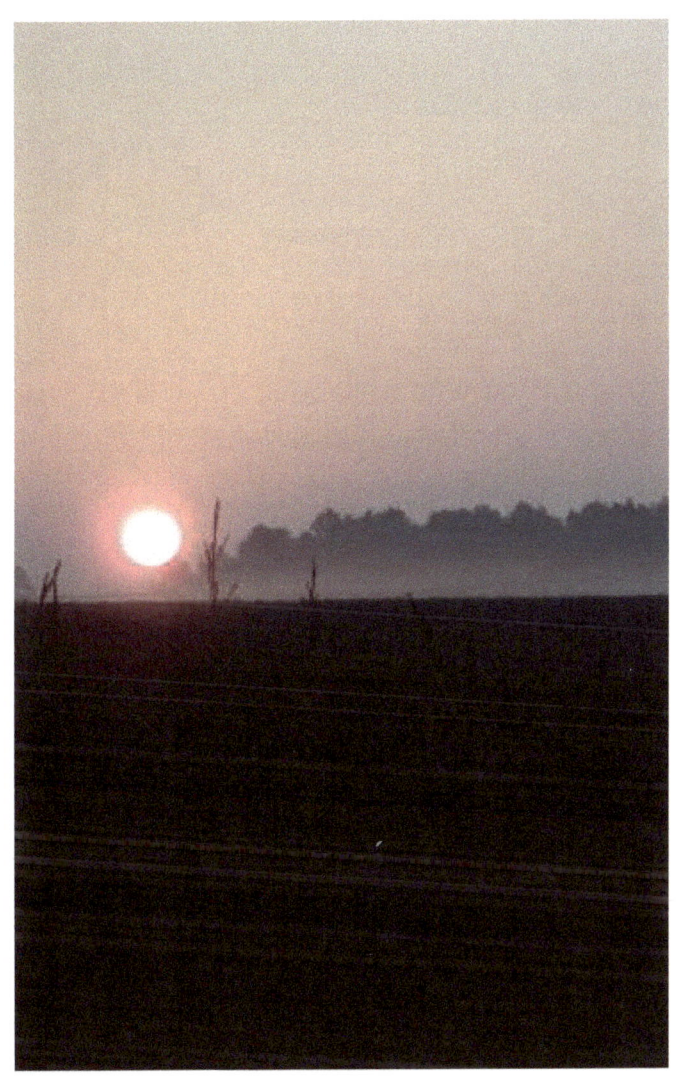

September Sunrise Through Mist

Often called American Mahogany, Chinaberry trees are found along roadsides and abandoned old farms. It is considered a useless trash tree with wood of no commercial value because the center of the tree often rots. I have sawed out a lot of this wood even though it yields less than 50%. The wood is brown, red, yellow and black. I use it for furniture and trim.

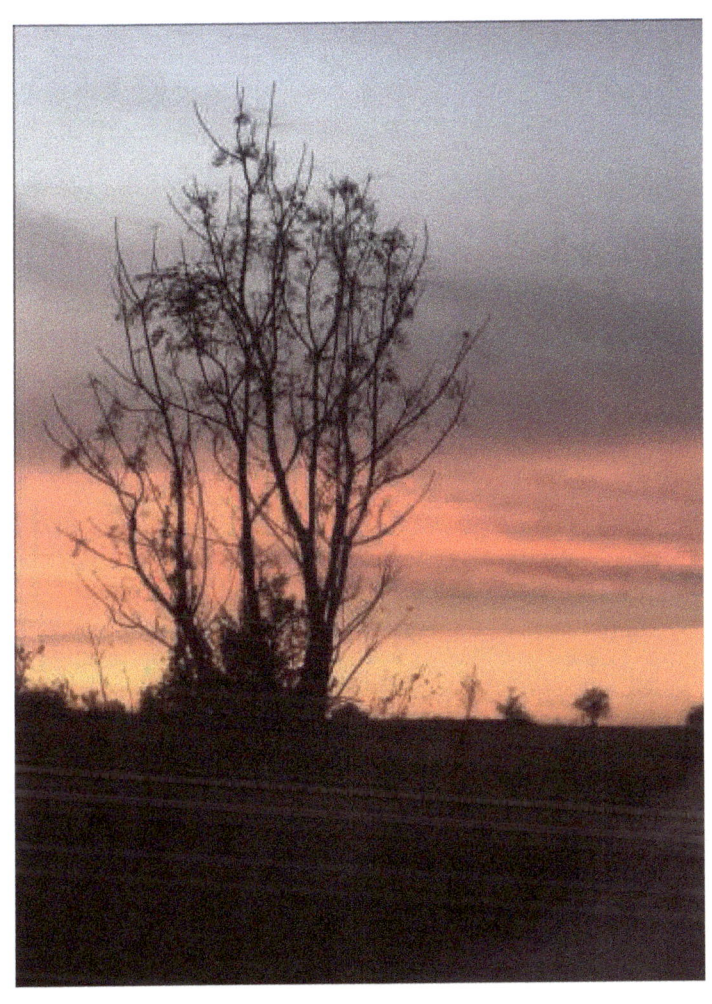

Chinaberry Trees

In early December a sycamore tree's leaves shine bright against the dark live oaks that do not lose their leaves until the spring when new leaves push out the old. A drowned oak from 60 years ago stands vigil in the pond.

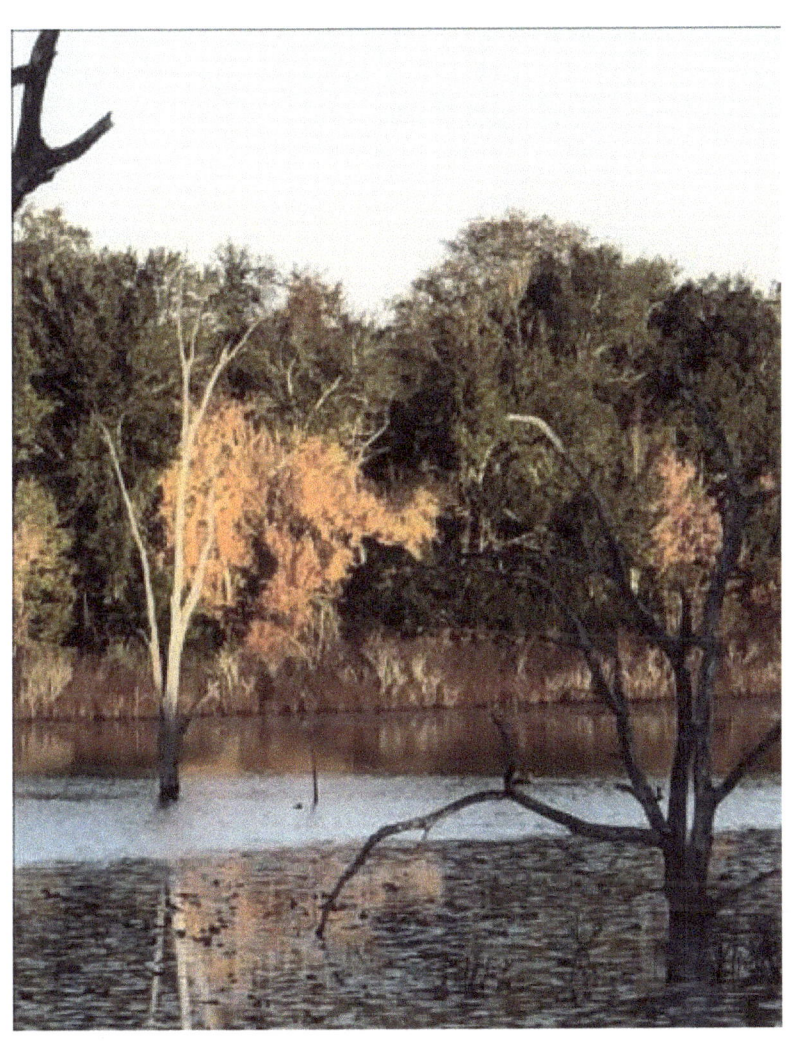

Autumn dawn on the Pond

Snow is rare in South Georgia. December and January host a few days of frosty mornings often with frozen fog. The sun quickly turns the silver frost into sparkling droplets of dew. Walking through frost coated grass produces a satisfying crunch that is all too rare in the south.

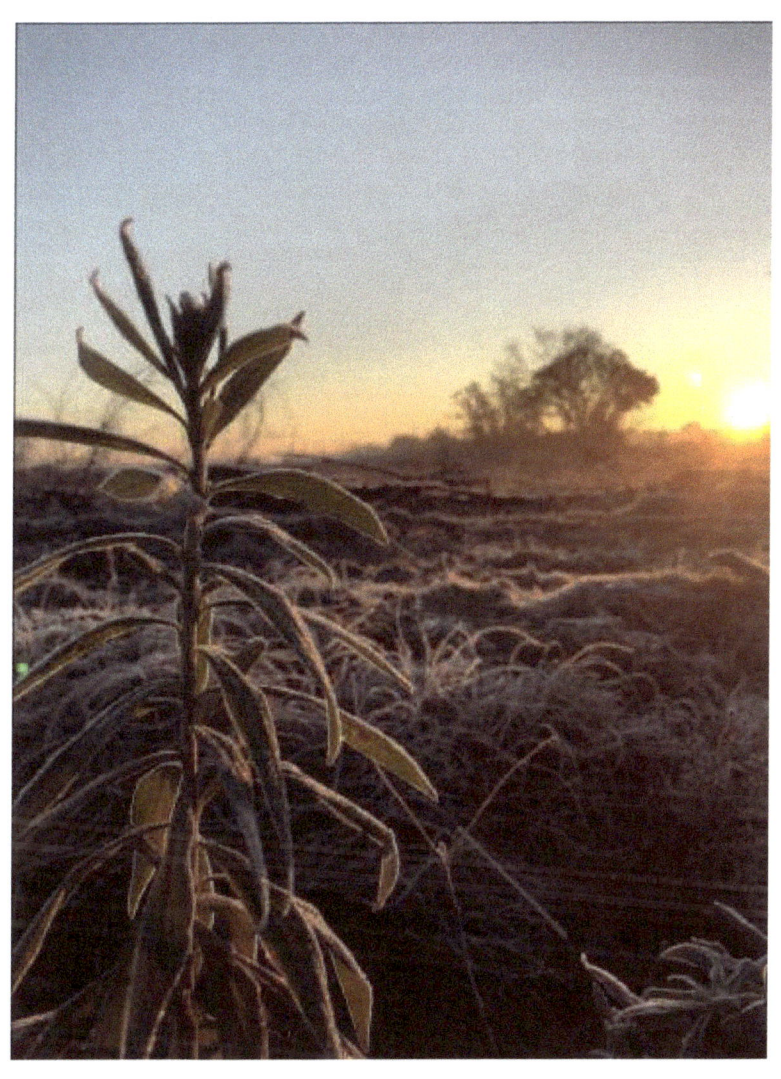

Christmas frost

A classic combination of streaming sunlight and pre-dawn darkness on my morning walk. Although the photo seems generic, the actual experience was quite satisfying.

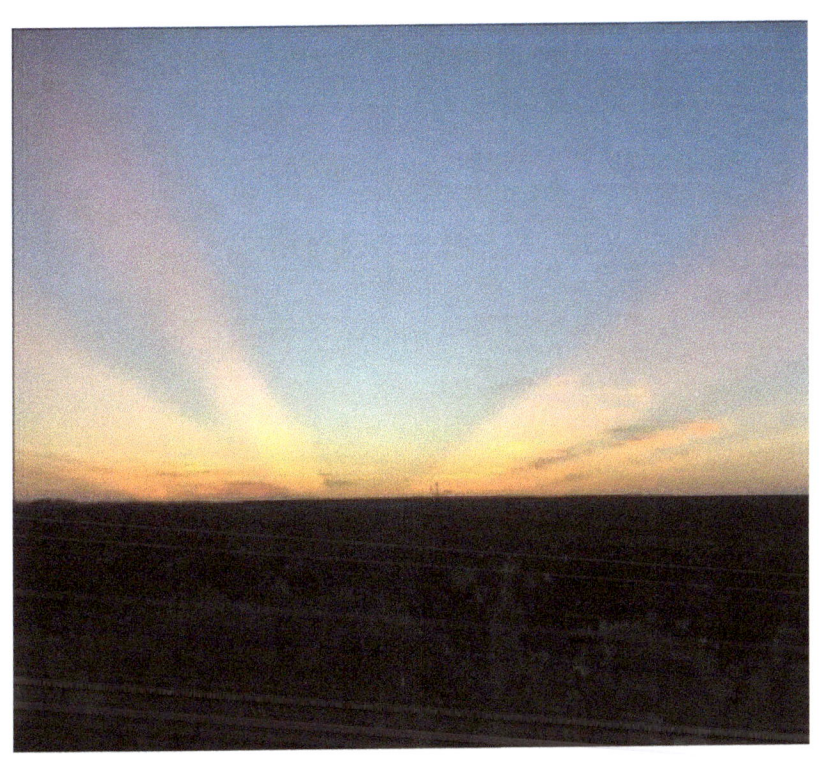

August sunrise

Cotton is a major crop in South Georgia along with peanuts and corn. On this morning I saw clouds, sunrise and sun dogs over the cotton field that waits the thresher. Or had our solar system spawned two new suns overnight?

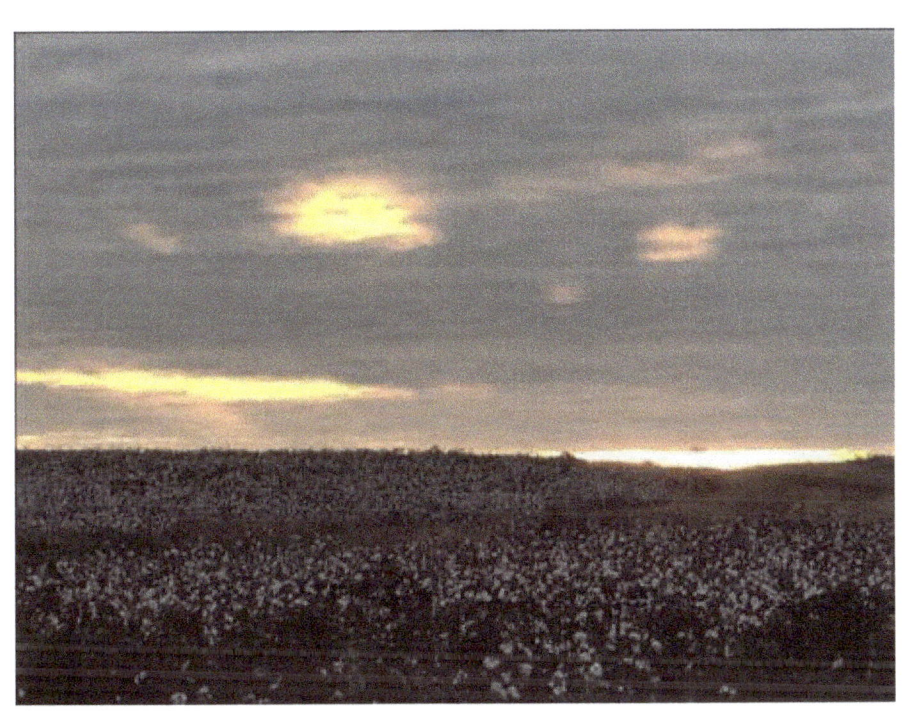

Cotton field and sun dogs

"Trumpet" flowers and poppies appear in late August and line the side of our dirt road with red, blue and yellow delights.

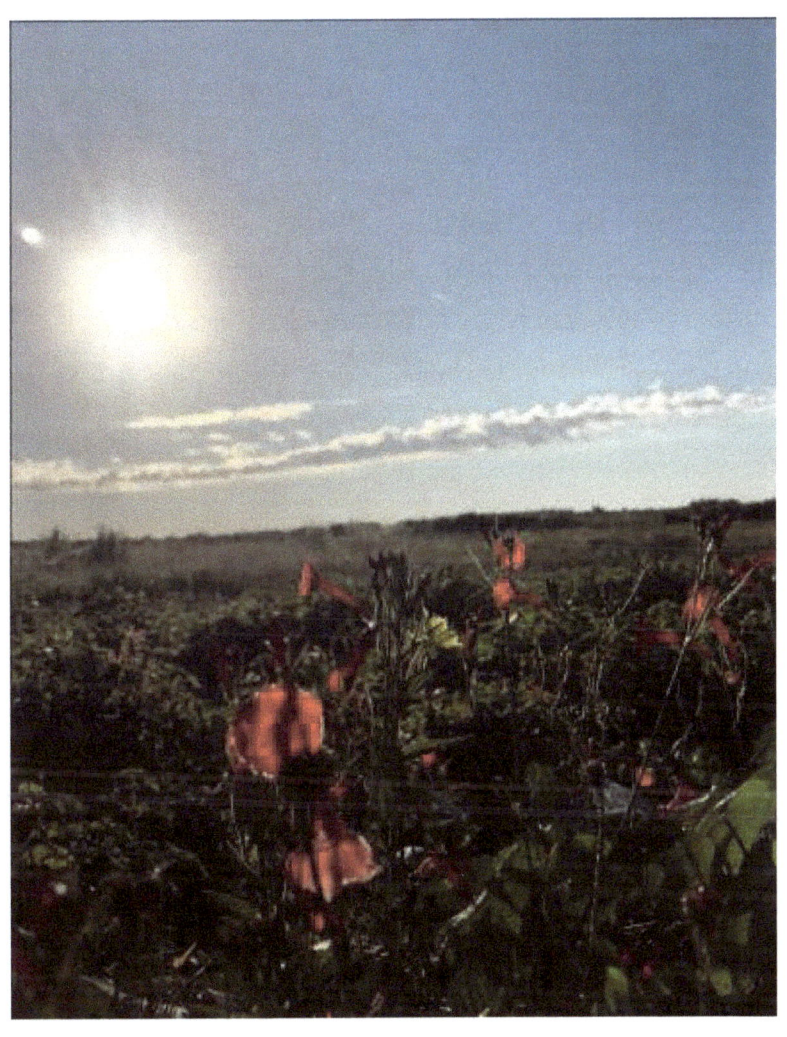

In the spring, pine tree woodlots are burned to reduce the underbrush and lower the chances for a destructive major fire. The pine trees with their thick bark are not injured by these minor fires. However, during the night with no wind the smoke settles on the ground like fog. Coughing and watery eyes.

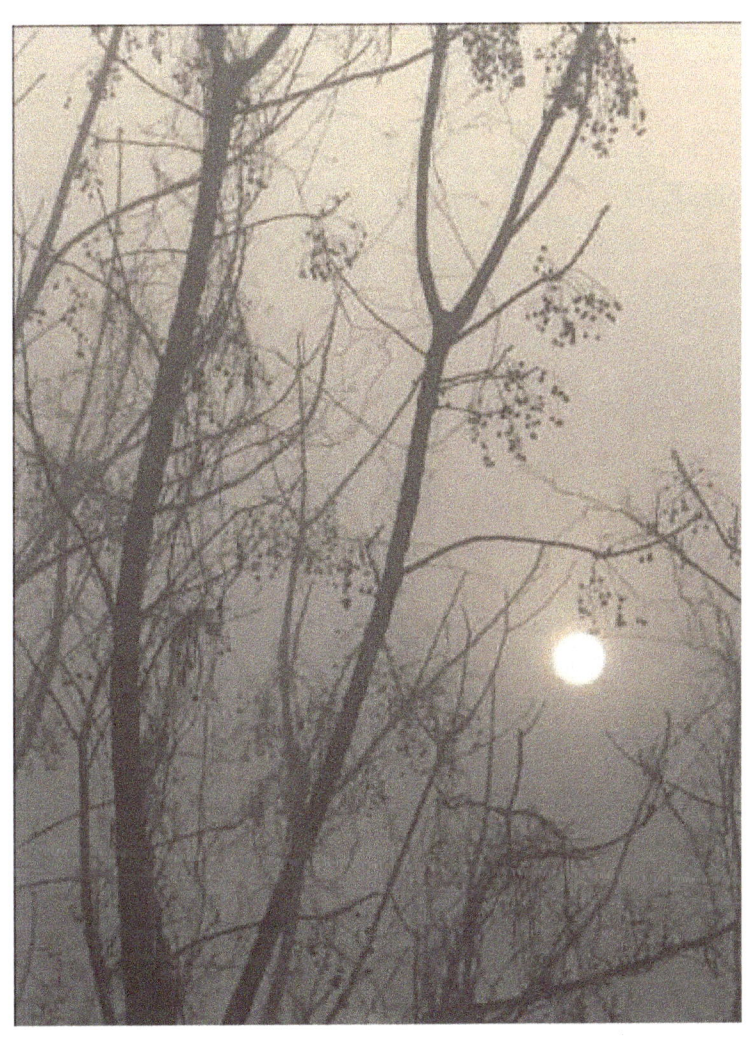

Smoke and chinaberry trees at dawn

Sunflowers stand like stoic druids facing east waiting for the sun god to bless them with growth and warmth. While only an occasional crop, they add a texture and color delight to the agricultural fields.

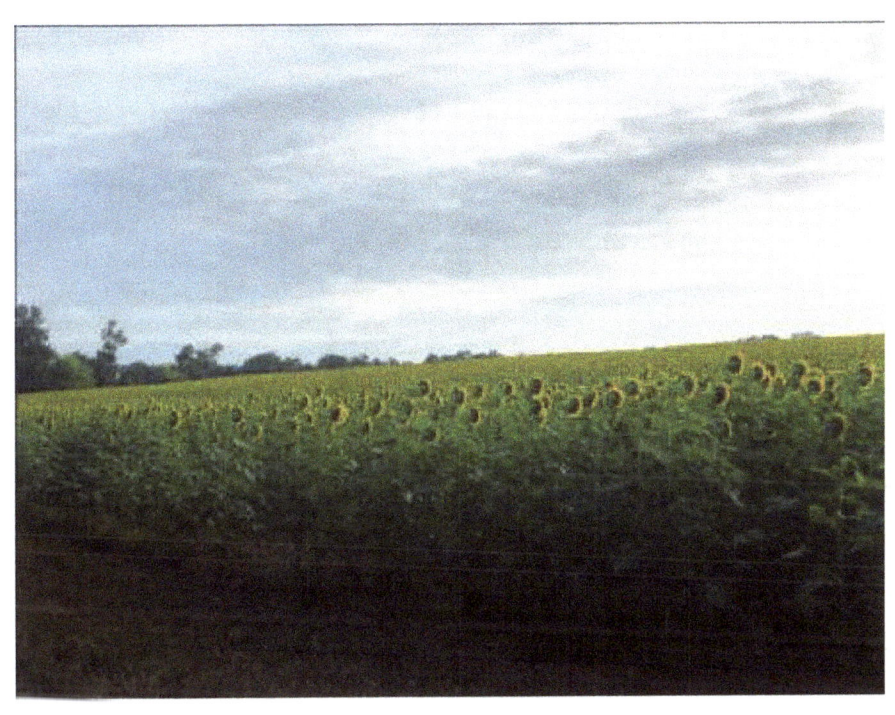

Sunflowers in August

A Morning Glory kissed by the sun. A promise for a lovely spring day in South Georgia. Behind, a dead birch tree reminds us that life rots quickly in the South.

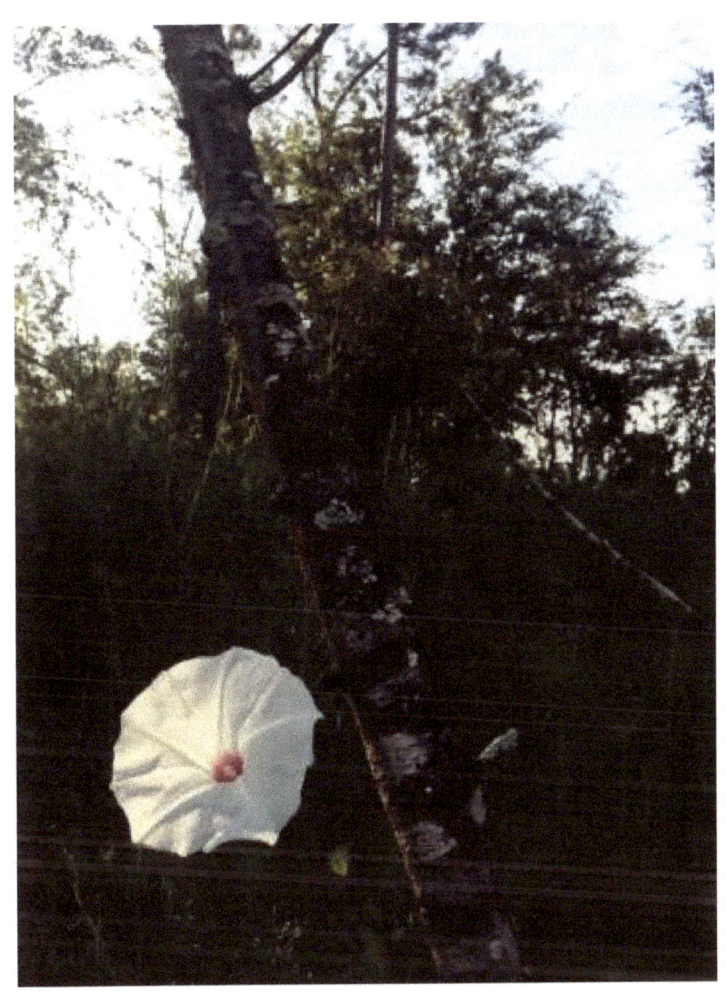

Morning Glory kissed by the sun

A few times a year in the mid-winter the shallow edge of our pond has a thin layer of ice that traps the water lilies. A few hours of his magic touch and the sun melts the ice.

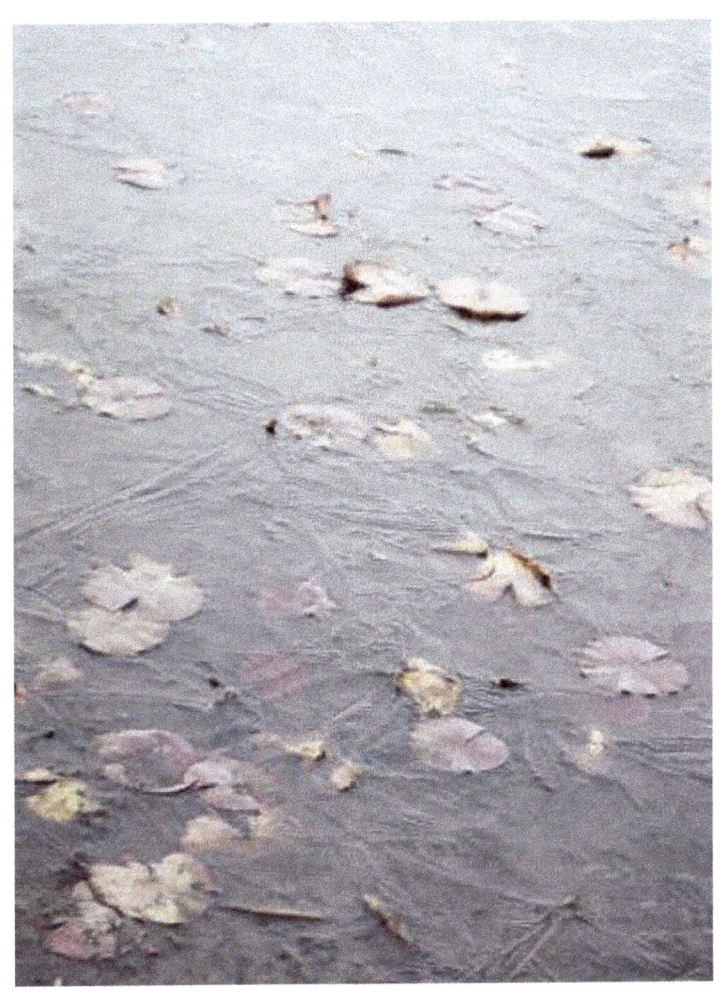

Water lilies and a frozen pond

SUNRISES IN OTHER PLACES

Dawn on Hinchinbrook Island National Park off the Northeast coast of Australia facing the Coral Sea. The 40 mile trail on this island along beaches, through forests, across streams with estuarian crocodiles, and straight climbs up waterfalls in full pack is considered one of the world's great hikes.

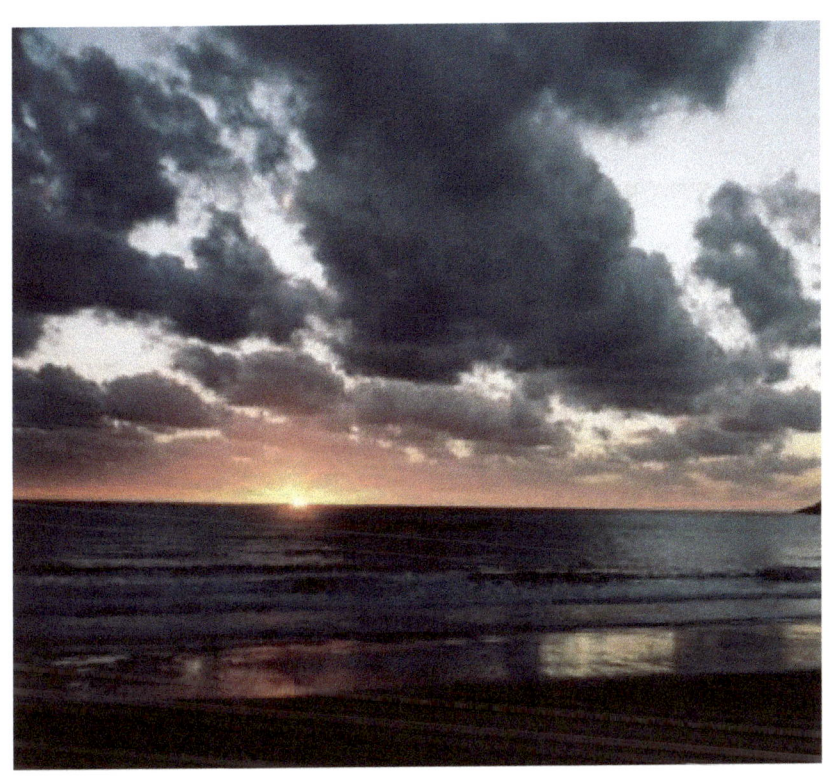

Dawn facing the Coral Sea

On the Middle Fork of the Koyukuk River above the Arctic Circle in Alaska. The sun never sets in early July. It skims the horizon with a faint appearance. Smoke in the distance from unchecked fires.

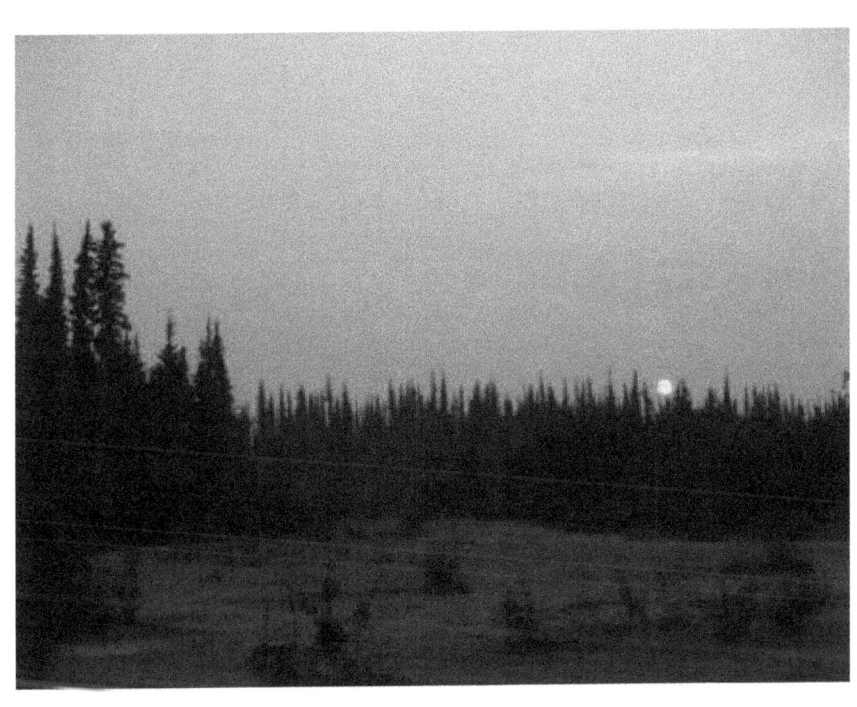

The Middle Fork of the Koyukuk River, Alaska

Dawn on the Noatak River in the Gates of the Arctic National Park above the Arctic Circle in Alaska. Barb and I canoed ten days on this beautiful river, camping on sand bars and hiking the mountains. Our first Alaska river trip.

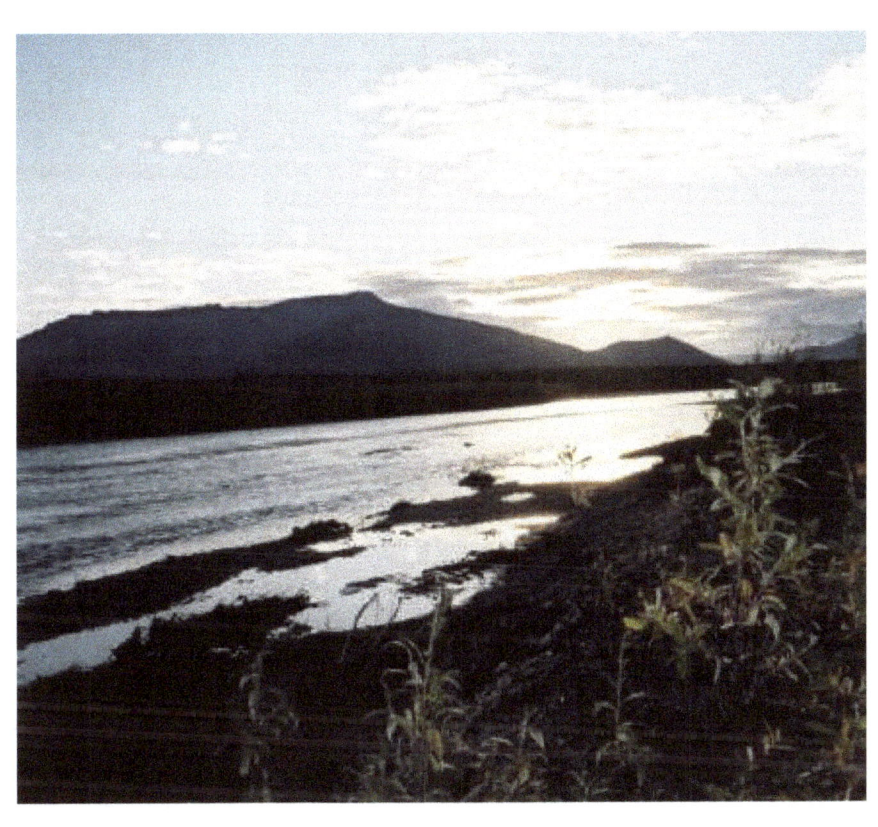

Noatak River, Gates of the Arctic National Park,

Above the Arctic Circle, Alaska

On the northeast corner of Glacier National Park in Montana is Chief Mountain. It marks the entrance to the Belly River Trail in what we consider the most beautiful national park in the lower 48 states.

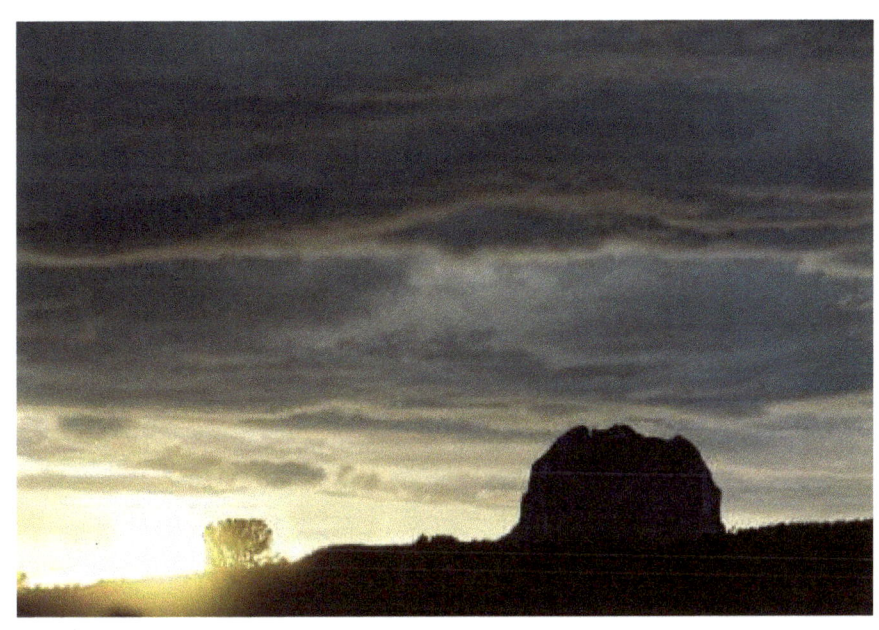

Chief Mountain, Glacier National Park, Montana

We hiked four days on The Brazeau River Trail in
Banff National Park, Canada to reach Brazeau Lake. A
morning of chill rain with snow on the surrounding
mountains. Too wet for a warming fire.

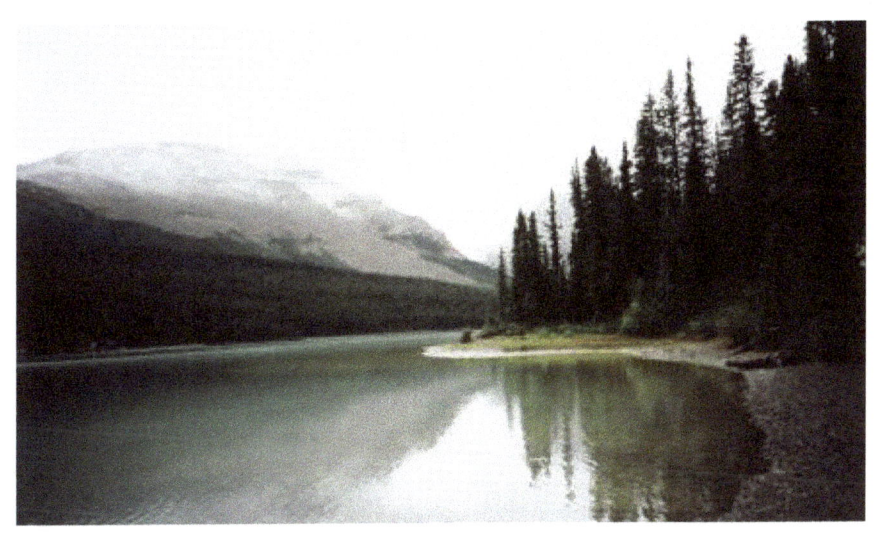

Brazeau Lake on the Brazeau River Trail, Banff NP, Canada

The Lanmanulauger Trail in Central Iceland goes through a sterile landscape of rheolite, lava flows, steaming vents, along glacier edges, and across cold-numbing streams. Considered one of the world's great hikes. Close to the Arctic Circle, the sun barely sinks below the horizon on a morning.

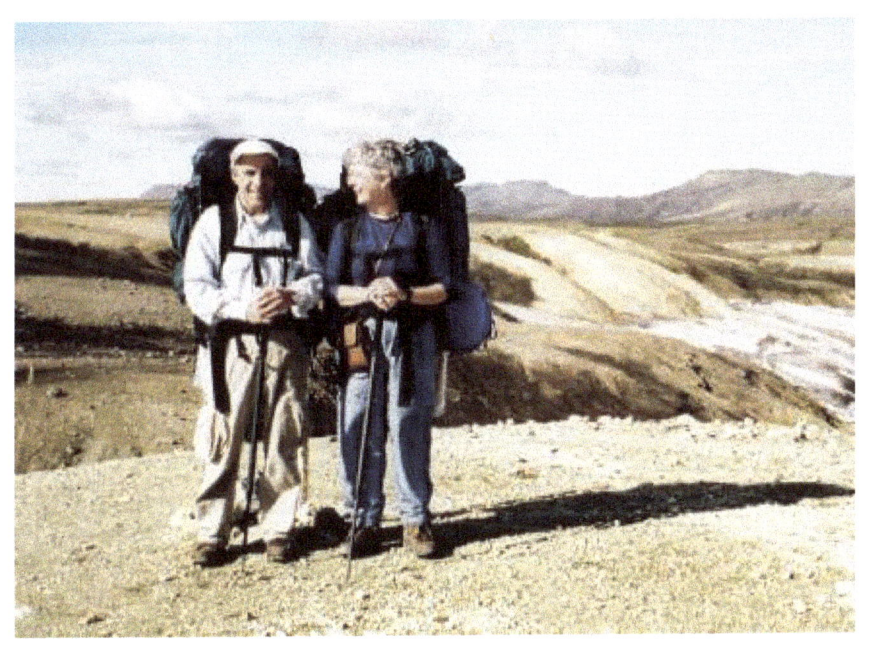

Lanmanulauger Trail, Iceland

Ireland's Dingle Peninsula is the greenest place we have ever been to. The Dingle Way circles the peninsula with its small towns, small pastures and endless sheep.

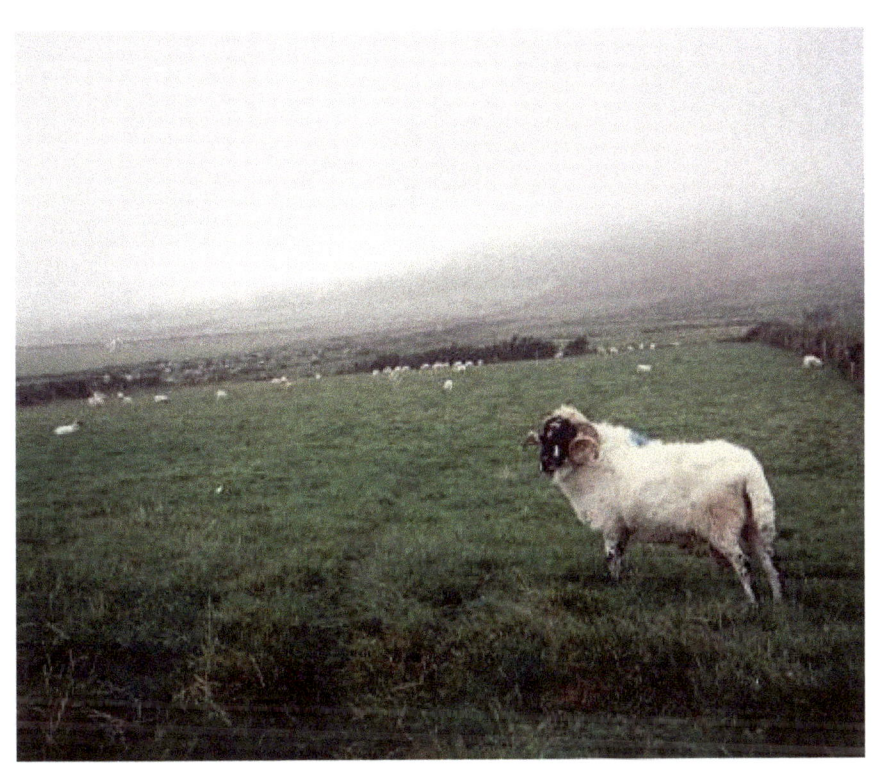

A foggy morning in Ireland

Tuscany, Florence and Sienna are Italy's gifts to humanity. One year we walked from near Florence to Sienna staying at farmhouses (agritourismos). Other years we did day hikes from a central Tuscan location.

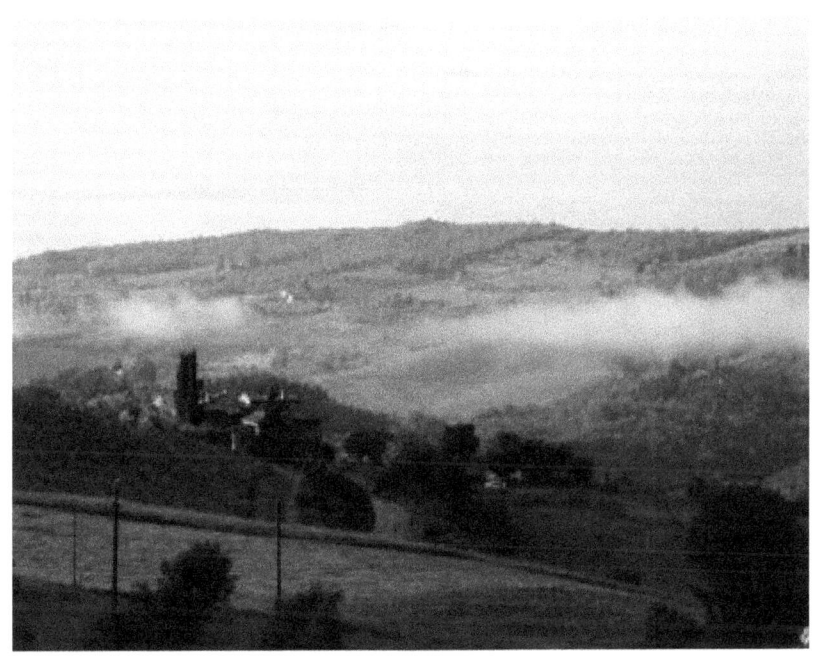

Foggy sunrise in Tuscany, Italy

The Little Missouri River in North Dakota is hands down the filthiest, muddiest river we have ever canoed. It traverses the state through the three sections of The Theodore Roosevelt National Park in the Badlands of North Dakota. The river derives its water from the Black Hills of South Dakota. By August the river is nearly dry.

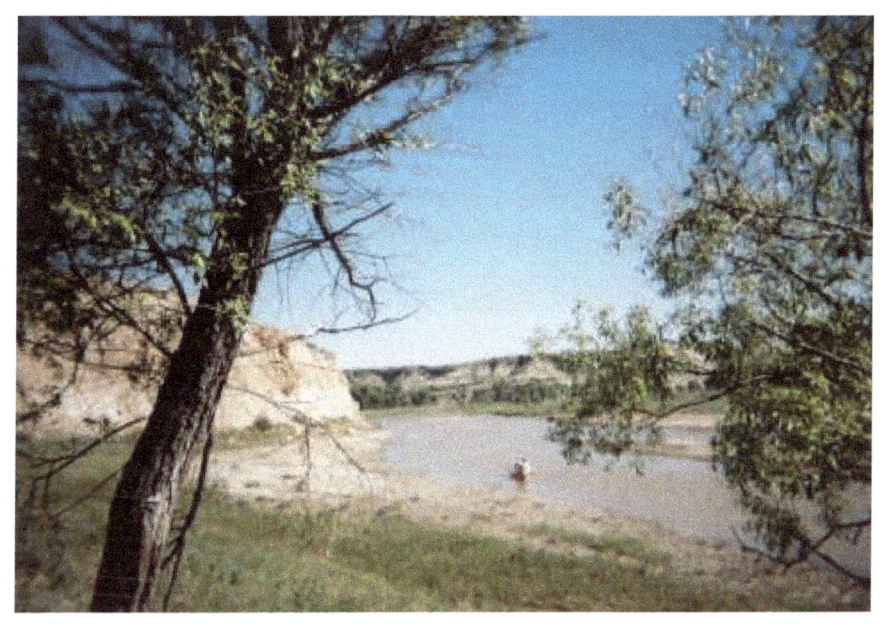

Canoeing at dawn on the Little Missouri River in North Dakota

The mighty Missouri River in Central Montana passes through the protected Missouri Breaks. We camped at the same places used by the Lewis and Clark expedition of 1804-6. Thick-barked cottonwoods line the river. Beyond the narrow riparian strip is a dry plain of minimal vegetation.

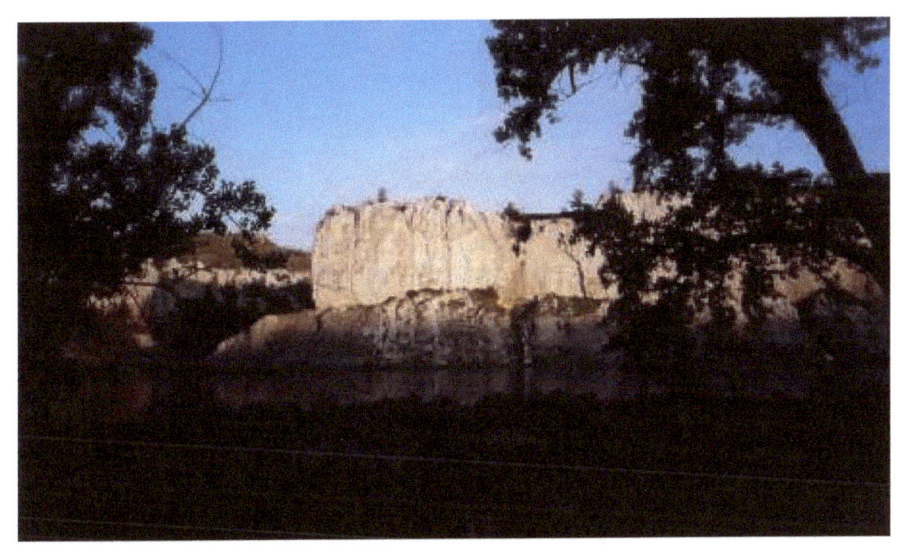

Missouri Breaks on the Missouri River in Montana

The one hundred mile Otago Bicycle Rail Trail ends in the once prosperous gold mining town of Middlemarch, South Island, New Zealand. Now, it is nearly deserted early in the morning. Not much more active at noon either.

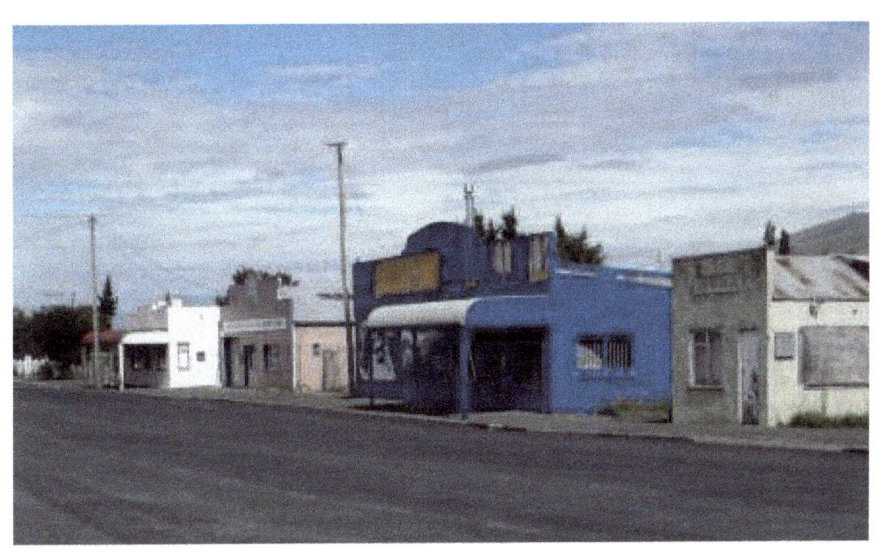

Middlemarch, New Zealand. Not much happenin'

Early morning on the South Downs Way National Trail in Southern England. A lone naked tree spreads its branches like a multi-armed skeleton.

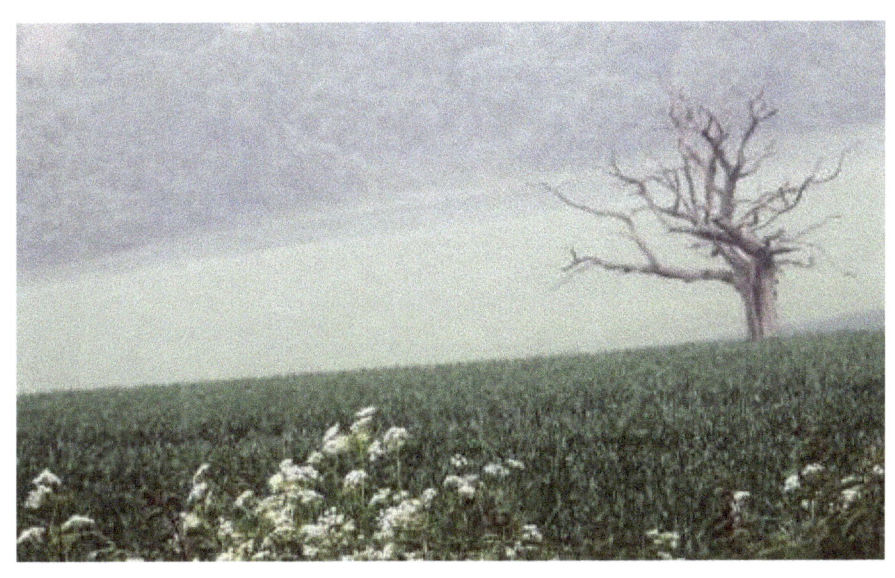

Ghost tree, South Downs Way, England

A multi-day November canoe trip on the fabled Suwannee River in North Florida. Camping on a sand bar along the red, tannin-stained river.

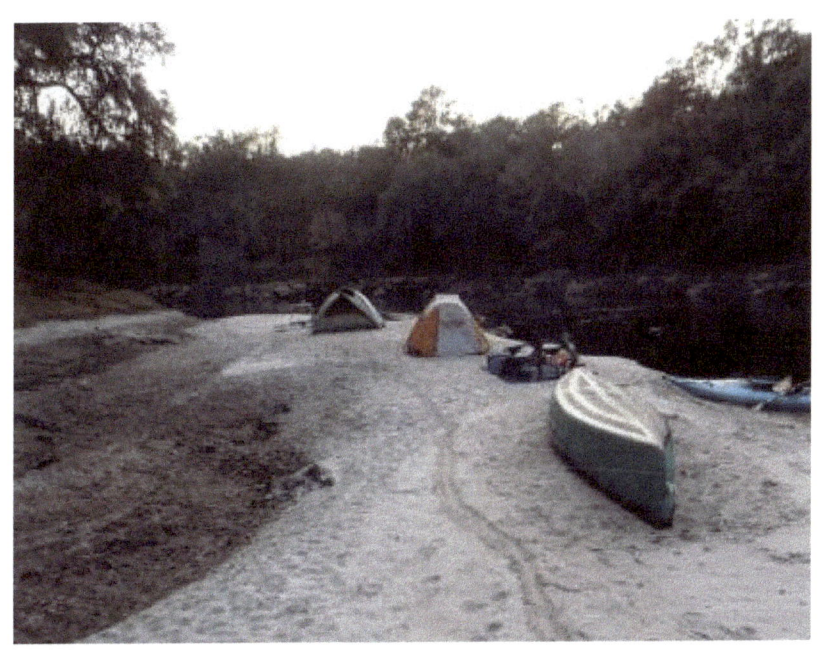

Rough camp on the Suwannee River, Florida

Empty, rugged Needles, Canyonlands National Monument in Southern Utah. Isolated patches of green growth line a trickle of water in the deep-shadowed Elephant Canyon.

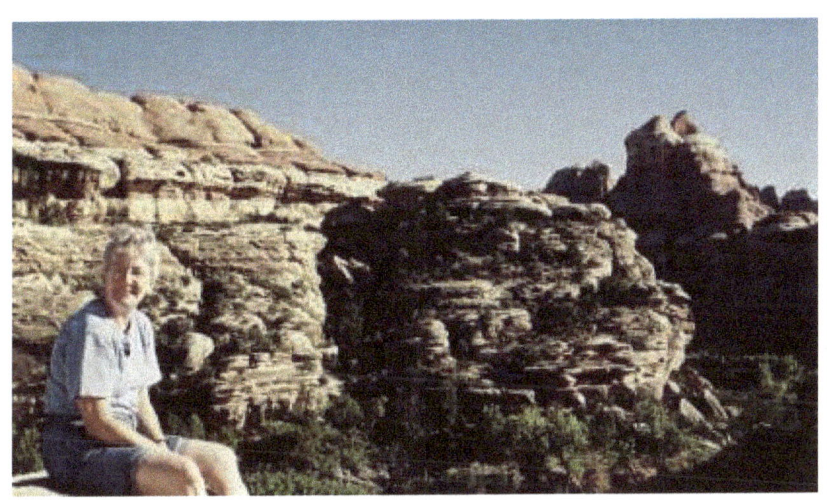

Needles Area, Canyonlands, Utah

The trail to Pinto Lake winds through a dense pine forest in Banff National Park, Canada. From there Matthew and I turned into The White Goat Wilderness where we saw no one for days and became wonderfully lost. At 8,000 feet in Cline Pass Mathew developed a nose bleed and my eyes throbbed with my heartbeats.

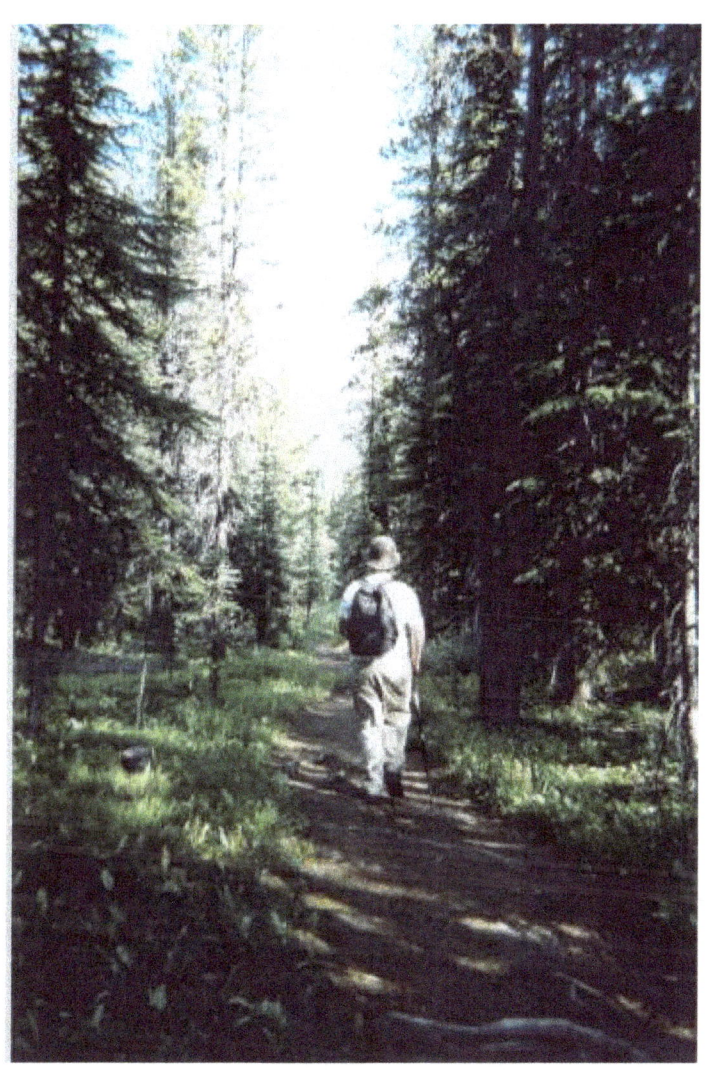

Trail to Pinto Lake, Banff NP, Canada

A morning fire from the ashes of one the night before. The Yukon River in Alaska from Eagle to Circle (160 miles) has an abundance of drift wood to make a fire for cooking and comforting. Just below the Arctic Circle, the sun sets for a few hours at night in July.

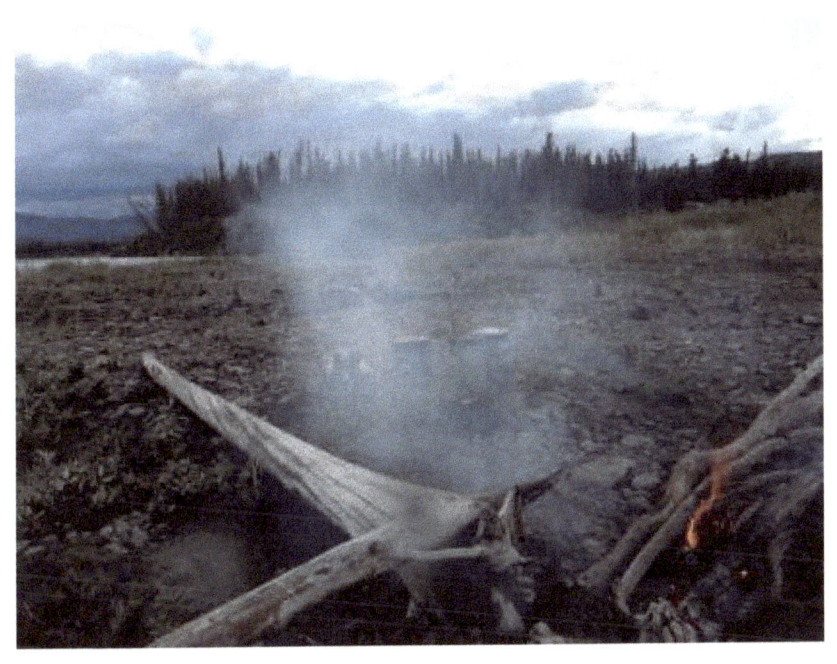

Morning Campfire on the Yukon River, Alaska

Alaska's Inner Passage is a long channel between the mountainous mainland and the mountainous barrier islands. Acceptable travel for me with my queasy sea sickness stomach.

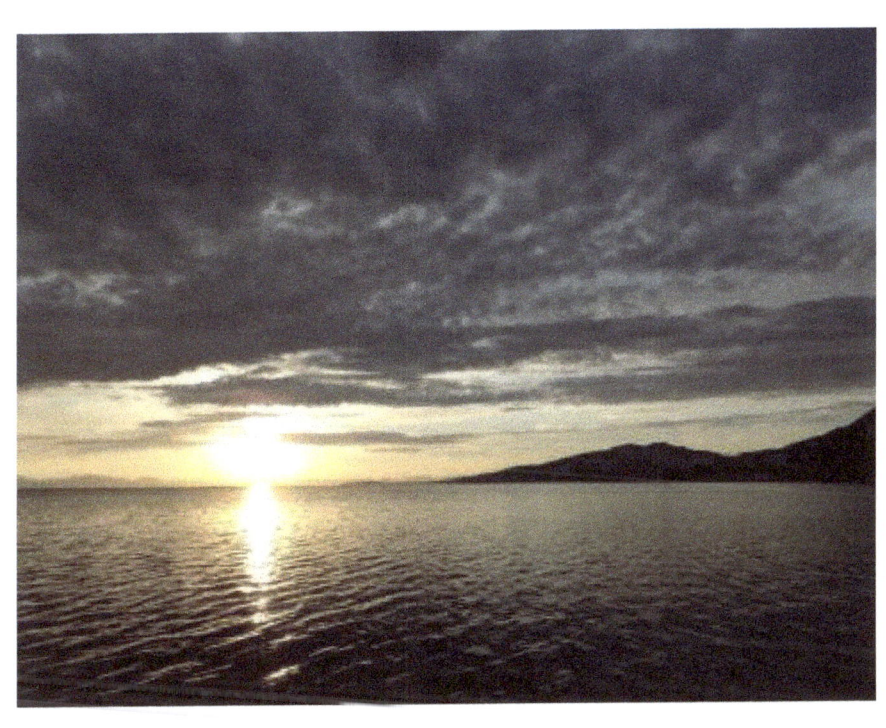

Dawn in Alaska's Inner Passage

A nine day canoe trip on the remote Kokolik River in the northwest corner of Alaska. At least 200 miles above the Arctic Circle the sun never dropped lower than about 20 degrees above the horizon. Even in June we had snow and ice in this treeless tundra.

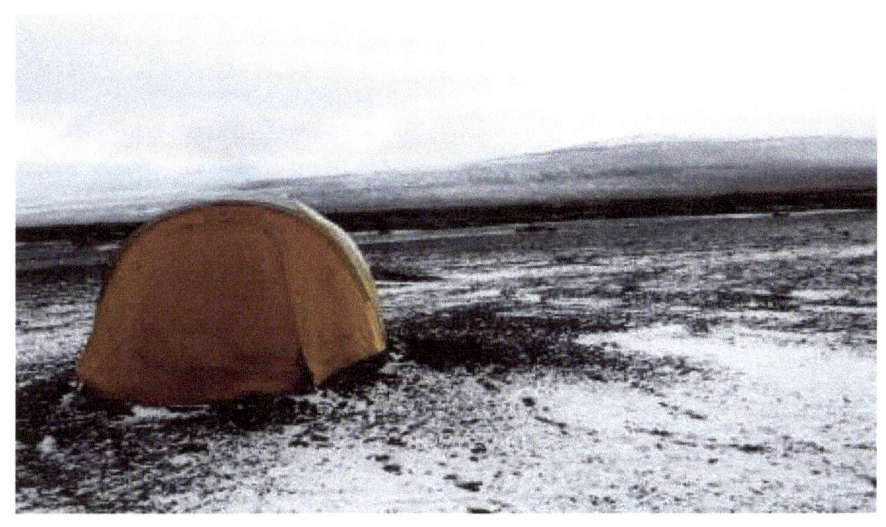

The Kokolik River, above the Arctic Circle, Alaska.

The Upper Peninsula of Michigan is a world away from the big cities in the south. Houghton was the heart of the copper mining industry eighty years ago.

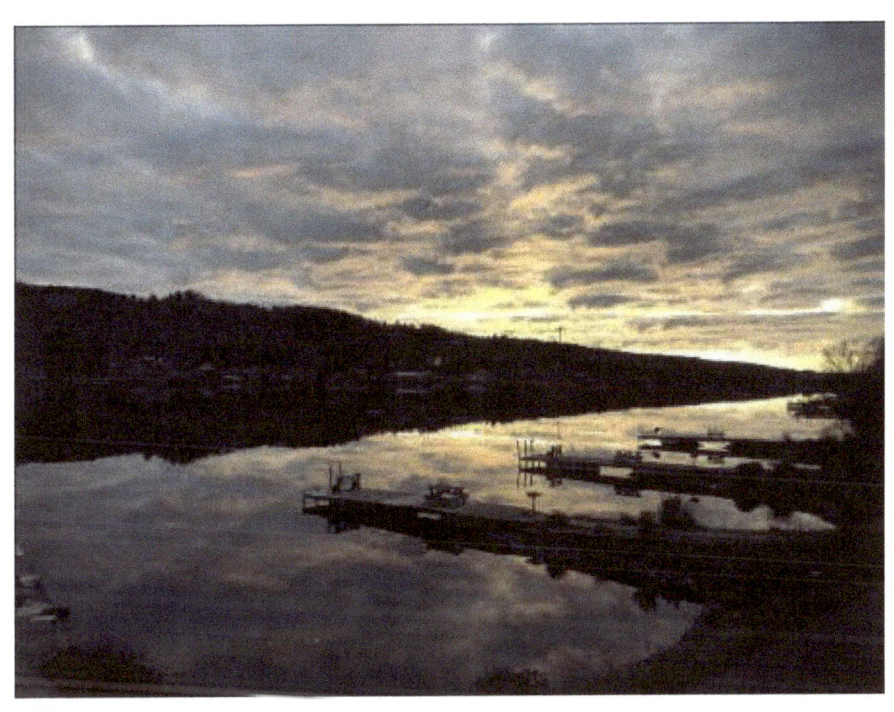

Houghton Michigan, Upper Peninsula

Millions of people view the Grand Canyon from the South Rim in Arizona. Less than ten present of that number go to the more rugged and beautiful North Rim. Uncontrolled fires filled the canyon with smoke that glowed in the slanting morning sunshine.

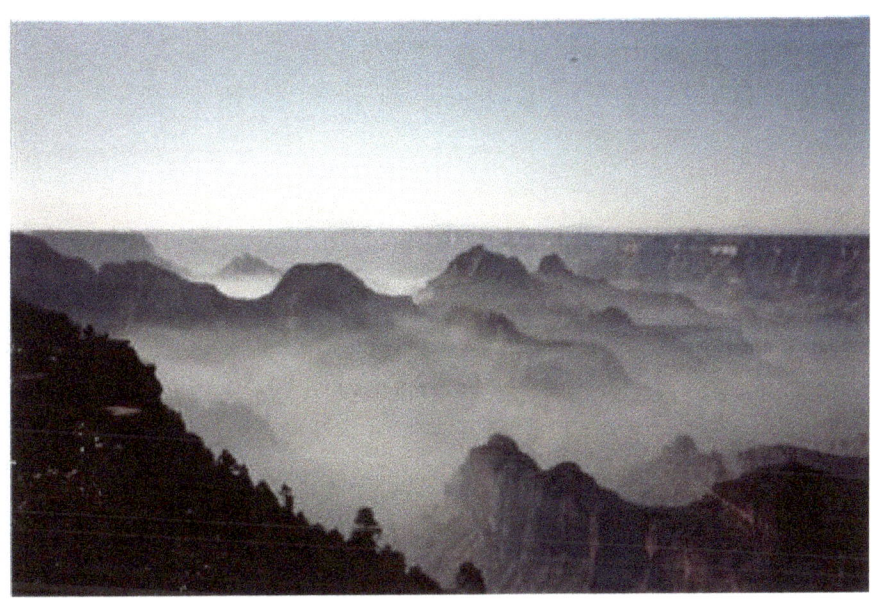

Smoke at dawn on the North Rim of the Grand Canyon.

Orange sherbet sky at sunrise over our lake. Early September after days of rain every afternoon.

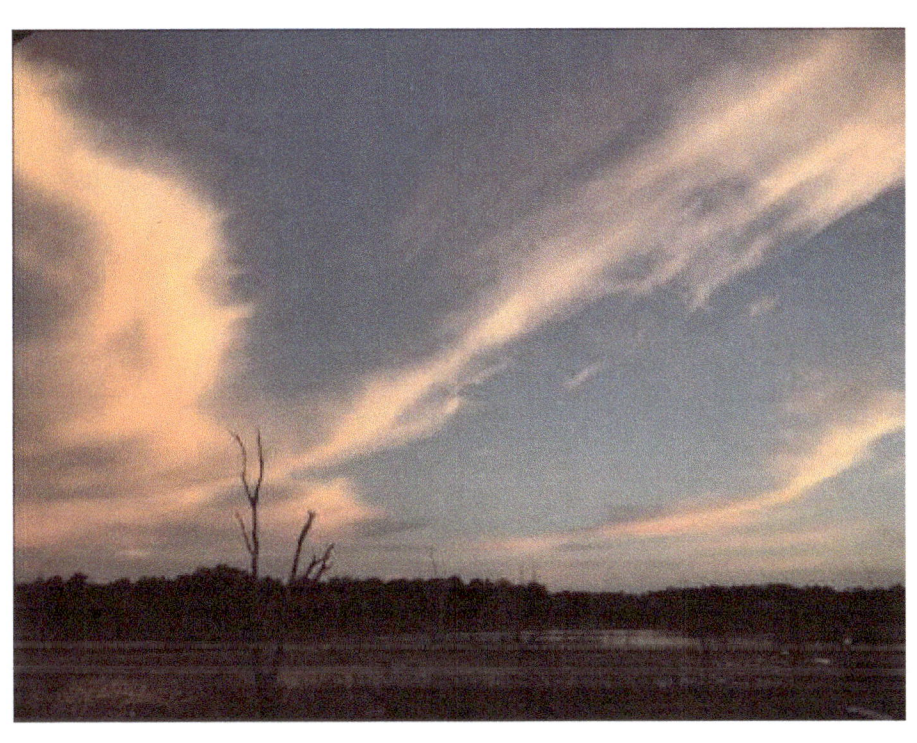

The small Mock Family Cemetery is our neighbor to the south. Its residents are quiet. Even on the morning after Halloween (All Saints Day) they don't disturb us.

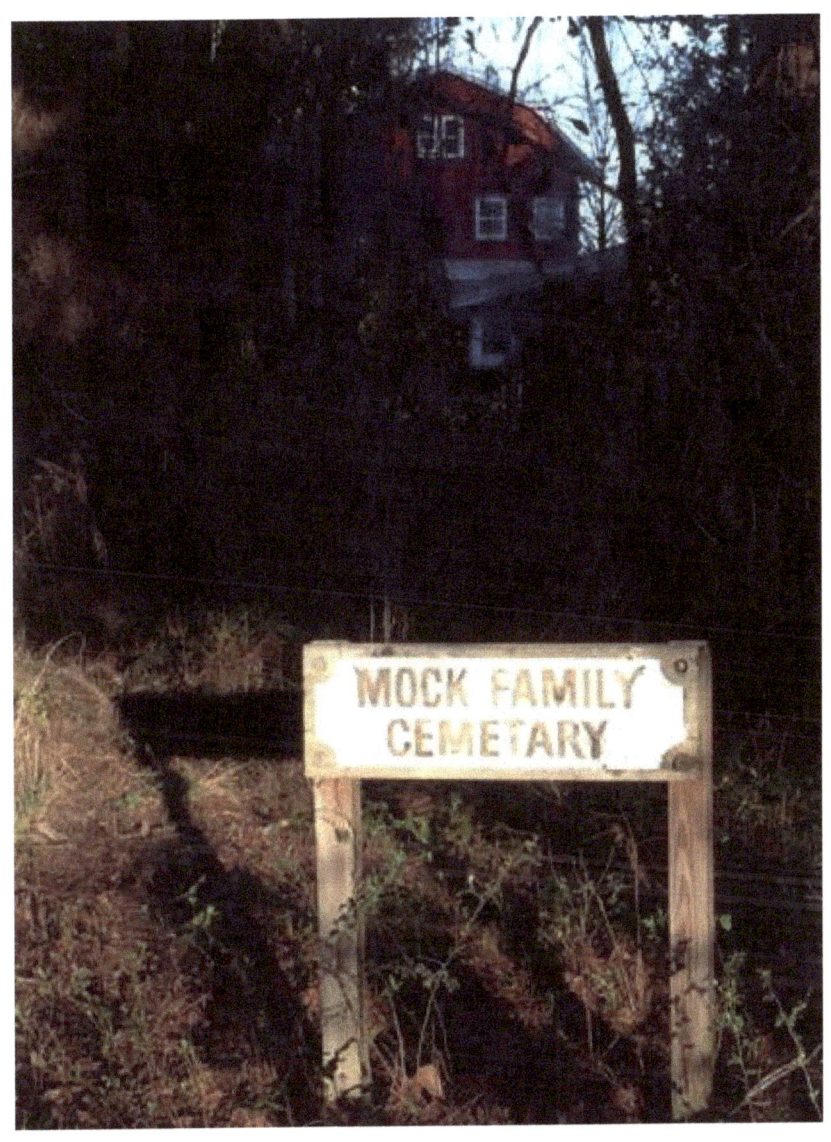

Around us are farmers' fields. In Bainbridge farmers mostly plant cotton, corn and peanuts. Occasionally a brave soul will try something different. Here the sun rises above a wheat field.

I hope you enjoyed this book of sunrises and dawns.

Paperback Books by Henry are available at lulu.com or at our website www.henryandbarbara.com.

Travel Junkies I, Parts 1 and 2

Travel Junkies 2

Travel Junkies 3

Travel Junkies 4

Travel Junkies 5

Travel Junkies 6

Travel Selections

A Trip to Alaska

160 Miles on the Yukon River

Canoeing Five Rivers in Alaska

Canoeing Six Rivers in Alaska

A Canoe Trip on the Yukon River from Dawson to Eagle (Almost)

A Canoe Trip on the Missouri River with Chip

A Canoe Trip on the North Fork of the Koyukuk River

A Canoe Trip on the Middle Fork of the Koyukuk River

A Canoe Trip on the Kokolik River in Alaska

An Un-cruise Through Alaska's Inner Passage

A Trip to New Zealand

A Walk in Wales on Offa's Dyke Path

A Walk on the South Downs Way in England

A Hike on Hinchinbrook Island, Australia

A Road Trip in Alaska and Yukon 1993

A Hike in Glacier National Park, Montana

A Hike in the White Goat Wilderness of Canada

Young and Single in New York City

Farm Days

The Trigamist

Anello and the Garibaldi Reunion

Anello and the Soldiers of WW II

Poems, Ghost Stories and Palm Readers

The Gloria Cycle: Good Evening Gloria's, Farm Days, and Yvonne

Two One Act Plays (The First Arrow and The Hippie)

Anello – A play

Under the Nurse's Cap

The Weenie Clinic

The I.M.P. Affair (Book and screen play)

The Adventures of Tony and Woof

Further Adventures of Tony and Woof

Tony and Woof at Uncle Henry's Farm

Recipes from Gloria's Restaurant

More Recipes from Gloria's Restaurant

The Making of a Cookbook

Ulysses Elijah – My Story

Oddments

How We Built Our House

Francois and Salvatore – Skits

Francois and Salvatore – Skits 2

Francois and Salvatore – Skits 3

Francois and Salvatore – Skits 4

A Comedy Evening 1 – The Rehearsal

A Comedy Evening 2 – Another Rehearsal

A Comedy Evening 3 – Still Another Rehearsal

A Comedy Evening 4 – The Last Rehearsal

Scrooge – A Comedy Evening

Two Holiday Plays

The Lost Mural of Ellis Island (with Andrew Sabori)

A Travel Photo Album

Travel Photos 2

Books and Plays by Basil Lucas Edited by Henry:

Eden

Not as the Crow Flies

Parade Rest

Royal Mess

Winter, A Boy

The Journal of Pokey Perkins

E-Books by Henry available at amazon.com and lulu.com:

A Walk on the Dingle Way, Ireland

A 100 Mile Walk on the South Downs Way in England

Canoe the Noatak River, Gates of the Arctic NP, Alaska

A Walk through Tuscany, from Florence to Siena, Italy

A Canoe Trip on the Missouri River, 100 Miles in Montana

A Canoe Trip on the Yukon River from Dawson to Eagle

A Canoe trip on the Middle Fork of the Koyukuk River

A Hike in Iceland on the Thorsborne Trail

A Hike in Needles, Canyonlands National Monument, Utah

Hike the Brazeau River Trail, Jasper National Park, Canada

A Hike in the Canadian Rockies, The White Goat Wilderness

A Hike on Hinchinbrook Island, Australia

A Bicycle Trip in Holland, Leiden to Haarlem.

Explore Alaska by Canoe and a Rent-A-Wreck Van

Ghosts, Spirits and Palm Readers.

Anello and the Garibaldi Reunion in Sicily

Anello and the Soldiers Returned From WW II

Exploring, Hiking and Biking in New Zealand

Ulysses Elijah – My Story

A Walk on Offa's Dyke in Wales

Scrooge – A Comedy Rehearsal

Kaikora Coast Track Walk

Otago Central Rail Trail

The Queen Ann's Way

Travel Junkies 1 - Part 1

Travel Junkies 1 - Part 2

Travel Junkies 2

Travel Junkies 3

Travel Junkies 4

Travel Junkies 5

Travel Junkies 6

Canoeing Six Alaska Rivers

New York City Days

The Adventures of Tony and Woof

More Adventures of Tony and Woof

Tony and Woof at Uncle Henry's Farm